THE SPIRIT OF AMERICA

Country Furniture 1700-1840
By Jerard and Pat Jordan

WH books

Published in the United States of America by
Wallace-Homestead Book Company
Des Moines, Iowa 50305

1

Photographers: Bruce Shultz, Thomas Warner

All furniture illustrated here is in the collection of the authors unless specifically acknowledged by a credit line.

ISBN: 0-87069-119-8

This book is dedicated to my parents who gave to me my appreciation of American history and to my wife, Pat, with whom that appreciation can be shared.

ACKNOWLEDGEMENTS

Our special thanks to all those who have made this book possible, especially to Mr. and Mrs. Frank Clear, Mr. and Mrs. Dana Fertig, Mr. and Mrs. Harry Fertig, Mr. and Mrs. Stephen Jones of Jones House Antiques, Mr. and Mrs. John Merkle, and Mr. and Mrs. Bruce Shultz.

FOREWORD

As an antique dealer and collector, I find that one of the most disturbing elements in the antique business is attempting to define what exactly is an antique. A simple rule of thumb would be that which is at least 100 years old. Such items technically can only be referred to as "late antiques" of the industrial revolution. Rather, I would like to feel that the true antique, besides evoking or preserving a way of living, also is a living demonstration of the work of man; i.e. what men have created over the years with their own hands and left for us to enjoy.

Often people have gone through our home and pointed to a given piece of furniture with the exclamation, "I really did not know this eighteenth and early nineteenth century country furniture was available to the public. The answer becomes both a yes and a no. No, it is not available to the average antiquer because that individual expects to purchase all antiques and especially those of early American origin with simple pocket change. That day has passed. Secondly, the answer is yes. Those pieces which are pictured in this book have been purchased over the last four years. For the most part they have been expensive; they have required many hours of searching over thousands of miles of roads, and numerous hours of study. The important fact is that quality, undoctored, American country furniture prior to 1840 is still available if one is willing to put an unlimited amount of time, effort, and study into the search.

The furniture throughout these pages is primarily country furniture as opposed to period. To that end one must look at each piece not simply as a bed, a table, or a chair, and leave it at that point with all the coldness which emanates from those labels. Rather, that bed, table, or chair must be looked at and appreciated as a piece of wood sculpture, created by a person who cared. With love and feeling, a utilitarian piece of furniture evolved. As one looks at a given piece, a certain amount of respect and reverence is felt, a pride in the American way is once again restored, and one can with great satisfaction state that this represents the SPIRIT OF AMERICA.

Jerard Jordan

Country Queen Ann Table

Sometimes, a piece is much more than just country furniture. It may carry with it that extra line, that minute, fine detail unique only to a particular craftsman, or some other very personal characteristic. Still, it may not be the sophisticated Chippendale, curly maple, slant-top desk. Rather it is a little bit of both the country and the formal — it becomes transitional.

Perhaps it would be helpful for the collector to become acquainted with the following chart which gives the approximate dates for period styles of furniture both in England and in America. Take special note that American furniture, as in any other form of artistic craftsmanship, was a partial adaptation of that style out of which it evolved (notably the English style of the time), and that extra craftsmanship which made it totally American. In Boston, New York, or Philadelphia, the cabinetmaker was concerned with the style of the period. The design was imperative or the product would not sell. On the other hand, the country craftsman was more concerned with a utilitarian piece for his own home. He adopted what was desirable according to his taste from the period furniture of the time, coupled this with his particular needs, and created a uniquely personal piece of furniture. Thus, American Country Furniture.

Period Styles of Furniture

Period Styles	Approximate Dates	
	England	America
Tudor	1558-1603	
Jacobean	1603-1649	
Cromwellian	1649-1660	
Carolean	1660-1689	
William and Mary	1690-1710	1700-1725
Queen Ann	1710-1720	1725-1750
Chippendale	1745-1770	1775-1790
Hepplewhite	1780-1790	1785-1800
Sheraton	1790-1810	1795-1815
Empire		1810-1840
Victorian	1830-1870	1830-1870

The pine tavern table (c. 1725-1750) shown here is of the country Queen Ann style. Rather pleasing to the eye, it is of simple design with a special note in the button foot and the thumbnail molding around the table top. Other characteristics are the dovetailed drawer, the long drawer pull and the 22" one-board top.

Courtesy of Mr. Dene King

In 1754, Thomas Chippendale, an English cabinet maker, published **The Gentleman and Cabinetmaker's Director,** which was dedicated to English furniture design. By 1775 to 1790 the Chippendale period predominated in American formal furniture, along with some country furniture. Shown is a country Chippendale tea table, attributed to Massachusetts. Of particular interest are the cartouche biscuit ends, and the deep, cyma-scrolled skirt which was a carryover from the Queen Ann period and commonly used in the middle colonies. In England the preferred wood was mahogany for Chippendale period pieces. Although this was used to a large degree in America, we find that walnut was quite prevalent, along with a simplification of design. The table represented is walnut (c. 1760-1775).

Pennsylvania Harvest Table

Courtesy of Mr. and Mrs. Bruce Shultz

While the early tables were of oak and usually long and narrow with a trestle leg arrangement, later tables took on any number of variations. Such tables as the bench table, the gateleg table, the harvest table, and others were made to be the most functional and to take up the least amount of space when not in use.

The table shown is a three-board-top, Mennonite harvest table from Lancaster, Pennsylvania. Dating around 1830-1840, it has several advantages over other larger tables. The construction is such that when it is not in use the three-board-top can be slid off the half dovetailed cleats, which through the use of pins hold it secure to the base.

The early craftsman had up to twenty-six varieties of wood to work with. Contrary to popular belief, oak was the most valuable wood with white ash second, especially in the making of tool handles and other items which had to be durable and yet strong. Walnut was valuable as a hard wood in the making of quality furniture, while pine and poplar were the most commonly used soft woods. Hickory became the best wood for the colonial fireplace, due to its warmth and illumination. Shown is a very fine walnut Pennsylvania farm table with nicely turned legs. The deep, wide, dovetailed drawer is unusual (c. 1820).

Shown here is a Pennsylvania country occasional table dating about 1830. Of specific interest here are the well turned legs, the breadboard ends and the dovetailed end drawer which is fairly uncommon.

Tavern Table

Courtesy of Mr. and Mrs. Joe Flegle

Several characteristics help in distinguishing a tavern table from other types. The earliest tavern tables had turned legs, at least one drawer, an "H" stretcher or a low stretcher on all four sides, possibly a breadboard end and a sufficient overhang on all four sides of a rectangular top.

One of the real problems in buying tables today is that, due to our generally being taller, we cannot sit comfortably at a table without our knees hitting the table skirt. Such was the case here until it was lifted on each foot about six inches. This in no way depreciates the value of the table. Mortised and tenoned throughout, of pine and from Pennsylvania, this table dates from the early nineteenth century.

Work Table

Courtesy of Mr. and Mrs. Frank Clear

Shown is a simple country Hepplewhite, scrub-top work table. Although not as early as the Hepplewhite period, it does date around 1820-1830. It was probably made for a specific place, evidenced by offset top and rounded corners. The terminology "scrub-top" is used specifically with tables. It means that the piece was primarily used around food and thus cleanliness was important. The custom was to scrub table tops with rather stiff brushes, thus over a period of time removing all of the original paint and retaining the natural patina. This has been the case here, while the base still retains the original red.

Night Stand

Courtesy of Mr. and Mrs. Frank Clear

Shown is a one-drawer, cherry, Sheraton style end table, more commonly called a night stand. Originally, it had a mushroom drawer pull. This table exemplifies the favorable construction point that the screws which hold the top to the base are set into a gouged out area on the underside of the table. Later construction procedures would not use that method. (c. 1800-1820)

Country Drop Leaf Table

In the country Hepplewhite style, this single drop leaf table dates between 1790-1810. The single-top board is its unique feature, measuring a full 27 ¼ inches. From Ohio, it retains the original red.

Shown is an unusual New England night stand in the original red. In the Hepplewhite style, this stand carries a four-sided shelf compartment as opposed to the usual drawer. Made from pine, it dates from around 1800.

Wash Stand

Courtesy of Mr. and Mrs. Frank Clear

About 1840 the idea of spool-turned furniture gained in popularity. Here is a typical washstand of that period displaying the spool leg, coupled with the cut-out back gallery and shelf. Notice the smaller drawer which seemed to be popular in the Mid-west.

Connecticut Candle Stand

Found in Connecticut, this stand of the early nineteenth century would commonly be called a spider leg candlestand. The legs and top are cherry while the rather heavy pedestal is maple. The top has the unique characteristic of a full inch, rounded corner board.

New England Candle Stand

This painted candlestand (1750-1790) with its urn-type pedestal would have enhanced any early home. Someone once stated that all candlestands which had dovetailed tripod legs were initially braced. That is not accurate, as bracing was done only as a supportive measure after age began to loosen the dovetailed joints. Unfortunately the legs of this stand show little refinement as compared to the more refined styles of the Queen Ann or Hepplewhite period. However, that makes this piece definitely country.

New Hampshire Candlestand

Out of New Hampshire comes this candlestand of the eighteenth century. The tiger maple rotary table, pine screw post and adjustable crossarms make this a very desirable piece. The advantage of the rotary table and adjustable crossarms was that of having the light at the most advantageous height under a given circumstance.

Bride's Box

One of the most interesting features of the seventeenth, eighteenth, and early nineteenth century homes is that of "accessory furniture," namely boxes. They were used freely, perhaps because they were rather easy to make, or they stacked easily taking up little space, or because of their utilitarian value coupled with decorative folk art. Within the home could be found candle boxes, chalk boxes, knife and fork boxes, hat boxes, salt boxes, pipe boxes, knife-scouring boxes, bride's boxes, along with an array of others. Pictured here is an eighteenth century bride's box which retains its hand wrought offset strap hinges, along with the original lock and key. The molded lid, along with the fine patina, creates a box of beauty and warmth.

New England Trinket Box

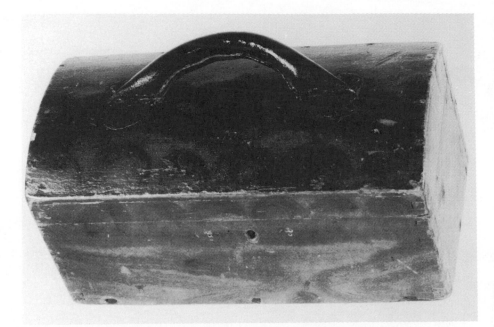

Symbolism and color were important to many of the ethnic groups which settled in America. We find the Puritans lining the inside of their coats in red. The Norwegians of Minnesota, the Dutch of Pennsylvania, the Cloisters, and numerous other peoples found part of their life in color. We are not suggesting that a home and all its furnishings were a conglomeration of colors and symbols, but one did find a generous use of blues, greens, muted reds, yellows and black, brought together in pleasing combinations.

The peacock was much used in decoration because of its multi-colors, for it brought warmth and happiness into the home. The tree of life symbol had an important kinship with the art of Persia which the Germans had been fond of since the twelfth century. The rooster stood for alertness. The many-pointed star expressed the spiritual struggle against evil. Other religious symbols were those of the angel, the heart representing God's love and hope, and the dove the bird of peace. Carried over from Europe was the lion which represented heraldry and the unicorn representing virginity. The Carolina parrot, a bird most hated by Pennsylvania farmers, was often used up through the 1840s when its existence ceased in Pennsylvania. Of greatest importance was the tulip which was a variation of the Holy Lily, representing the promise of paradise. Its three leaves denote the Trinity. At times there was no esoteric significance to the symbols. They were drawn and painted just because the people appreciated them.

Pictured is a smoke decorated, New Hampshire trinket box. It is unique because of its leather heart handle. It was possibly made by a bridegroom for his new bride.

Candle Box

Candles are simply a matter of purchasing today, but there has not always been such easy accessibility. The early settlers who desired to burn candles had to make those candles. Often one had a choice of making tallow candles from beef or mutton fat, bayberry candles from the bayberry shrub, or wax candles from bees wax. Tallow candles were probably the most common for the home, whereas bayberry and beeswax candles were usually saved for special occasions. Since candles were a luxury and expensive, unused candles were safely set aside in a protective candle box until they were needed.

Shown is a pine, double candle wall box of the mid-nineteenth century. The bottom compartment was for the new candles while the top compartment kept those burned stubs which would later be remelted and dipped.

The miniature chest pictured represents a true piece of New England or Pennsylvania folk art of the early nineteenth century. Employing the use of "line carving" (impressed design as opposed to "chip" design), the back and right side are decorated. The geometrical design on the left side and front has been "chip" carved along with the inside till cover. Two chip carved rosettes on the front are a type of simple Friesian carving practiced along the Atlantic seaboard. A drawer extending the complete length pulls out from the left side via twisted wire pull. Signed D.M. 1830, it is pegged throughout. Originally the top was hinged through the use of two tin strap hinges with a hand-wrought lock clinched through the lid. Overall measurement is 7" long x 3¾" wide x 3¾" high.

Double Arch Candle Box

Here is a very fine eighteenth century, double-arch candle box retaining much of its original design. Small hand-forged nails hold the mitered corners together.

Slide Top Candle Box

Another type of candle box had a slide top. This fine example from the early 1800s retains its original stenciling on the four sides, while the slide is hand painted in a flower motif. For practical purposes one can use the date of 1815 as the beginning of the stenciling period.

Salt Box

Pennsylvania Amish salt box of the mid-nineteenth century. Notice the cutout geometric design.

A knife and fork wall box from Rhode Island. It is unusual to find this type of box with a lid and in the original green. (c. 1840)

School Box

On this pine hand decorated box, note the great detail in the center rose and the two side rosebuds, along with the fractur type initialed lid. Only 9 ½ " x 5 ¼ " x 5 ¼ ", this piece of folk art has a twisted wire hook and catch along with cotter pin (staple) hinges. Judging from the staple hinges, the fractur lettering, and the rose head nails, the box is probably of Pennsylvania-German origin and made between 1790-1820.

Wood Boxes

The woodbox, usually of the simplest design, carried with it one of the most important aspects of the country home. It was the woodbox which held the wood for the fireplace or wood burning stove. And it was of utmost importance that it be always full, for the family lived around the fire. The fire heated the home in the winter and cooked the meals all year around. The first chore a young child would have would be to keep the woodbox full.

Basically, there were three types of woodboxes with numerous variations. The simplest would be the open top such as the Ohio woodbox pictured. Decoration was usually minor, so this one in the original blue with the designed headboard and sides is rather unique. Occasionally one finds a woodbox with a drawer either at the base or top.

A second type of woodbox would be the closed woodbox with either one or two compartments. When the top was down it made a rather hard seat, but in those days nothing was really what we would call comfortable today.

The third type would be the woodbox settee, which was designed both as a woodbox and a seat. From Pennsylvania, the one shown, in the original red, probably sat on the side porch close to the kitchen. It has two inside compartments, one for kindling and the other for larger logs.

One of the most interesting woodbox settees I have ever had the opportunity to own is the double, early eighteenth century, Pennsylvania piece shown above. The hand-painted design on the top back board, the unusual shoe-type foot, the arrow back with ball bottom, plus its being dovetailed, mortised and tenoned throughout make this piece very desirable.

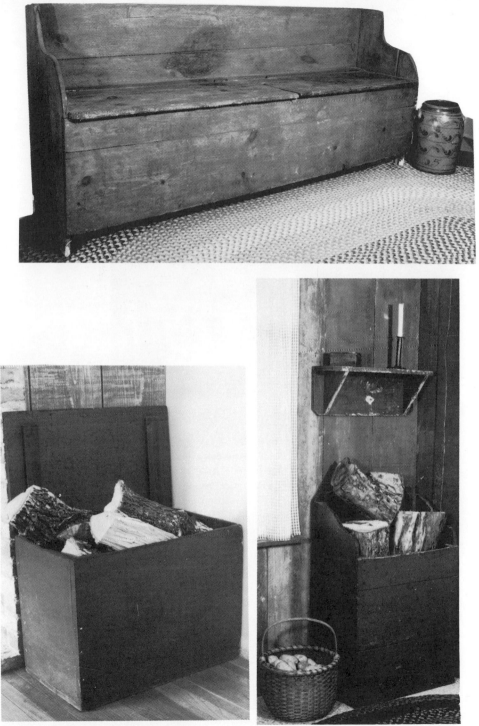

Courtesy of Mr. and Mrs. Frank Clear

Pilgrim Century Slat-Back Arm Chair

The chair, like the table and other basic furniture, can be placed in the same period categories which were outlined earlier. However, there is a great deal more in the identification of a chair as to its type than simply to state it is Queen Anne, Chippendale, Tudor, or whatever. The basic period must be broken down. For instance, if it is of the Pilgrim century, is it in fact Carver (named after John Carver, selected governor of the Pilgrims at Plymouth in 1620)? Or is it a Brewster chair (Elder at Plymouth until 1644), which had up to forty spindles on the back, side, and front of the chair? If one has a Windsor, is it a fanback, comb-back, or continuous arm?

Categorical generalities have no place in determining furniture types. The art of collecting country or period furniture is one of knowing exactly what a piece of furniture is and how it was made. What does the style indicate? What about the finials and feet? Is it completely original or has it been restored? Approximately what is the date? All this plus more is important to the piece and also to its value. Secondly, is it the best possible piece which you can find and buy for the money? Will it appreciate in value or will you have to apologize for it and take a loss. One rule to keep in mind, both for the collector and the dealer, is to spend the extra money and buy only the best.

Pictured is a Pilgrim century, slat-back arm chair dating between 1700-1720. The front, the arched slat back, the rolled arms, and especially the ball feet indicate its Pennsylvania origin, more specifically of the Delaware Valley.

Pilgrim Century Slat-Back Arm Chair

This Pilgrim century, slat-back arm chair dates between 1680-1710. Notice the sausage and ball turned uprights combined with the arched slats and the simple stretchers.

During the late eighteenth century, Mother Ann Lee brought to America the religious sect known as the "United Society of Believers in Christ's Second Appearing." Commonly known in America as the "Shakers," they founded their first community at Watervliet, New York. Today only a handful are still alive, living in the community of Sabbath Day Lake, Maine.

The nineteen Shaker communities for the most part were self-sufficient, including the producing of their own furniture which had a style of basic simplicity demonstrated in these pictures. The chair on the left was made at the Shaker Society, Alfred, Maine, about 1820. To the right of the sugar chest, is a chair made around 1830 at Sabbath Day Lake. Both chairs have split ash seats.

It would be incorrect to state that the Shakers were not aware of style changes in furniture. This cherry chest from Pleasant Hill has some Sheraton characteristics, especially in the legs. (c. 1820)

Shaker Ladder Back

Courtesy of Mr. and Mrs. Harry Fertig

Made by the Shakers at the Alfred, Maine, community, this chair is unusual in that it retains the original leather seat. (c. 1820)

Prior to 1720, the Windsor chair was made in and around the town of Windsor, England, most likely to the north in High Wycombe Shire. By 1720 we find the joiners of Philadelphia creating the first American Windsor. Of interest is the fact that the chair was originally advertised as a garden chair which would be relegated to the storeroom or the attic if one were entertaining. Only in the less wealthy homes would one find a Windsor in the sitting room. Being a garden chair, it was usually painted green, later colors being red, white, yellow, and occasionally black.

An important characteristic of Windsors is the continuous arm with New England turnings. The turned legs could be of several styles, including the turned bamboo of the early nineteenth century. The arch back of the continuous arm shown is of green ash which has been split rather than sawed so that all the wood fibers are continuous throughout the entire length. Green hickory and white oak were also used. The stretchers were usually of maple, while the seat was of pine with a slight chamfer on the leading edge, cut away underneath to give the impression of lightness. Notice also the pronounced saddle peak at the center front of the seat which adds to its comfort. This continuous arm dates around 1760-1770.

The American Windsor is distinct from the English because of several construction techniques. First, the American saddle seat, because it is chamfered and the underside is cut away, is less heavy looking. Secondly, the spindles will be either New England, Philadelphia, or bamboo, as opposed to a simple unesthetic spindle. Thirdly, the slant leg on the American Windsor will have a greater splay than the straight leg of the English Windsor. A fine example of the American Windsor is truly a chair of grace through design and craftsmanship.

The Windsor pictured is representative of the period 1790-1820 when bamboo turning was popular. Note the slight saddle seat, the slightly splayed bamboo turned legs and the arm decoration, all of which lend to its beauty.

Daniel Lawrence Windsor

In 1787, the Providence, Rhode Island, paper carried the following advertisement:

"Daniel Lawrence informs the respectable citizens that he carries on the chair-making Business in Westminister street where he makes and sells all kinds of Windsor Chairs, Garden Chairs, also sofas, settees, etc. in the newest and best Fashion, neat, elegant and strong, beautifully painted, after the Philadelphia mode, warrented of good seasoned materials, so firmly put together as not to deceive the Purchaser by any untimely coming to pieces."

The advertisement was correct — for here two hundred years later, is a continuous arm Windsor signed Daniel Lawrence.

Courtesy of Mr. and Mrs. Stephen Jones

A very fine eighteenth century New England turned, Rhode Island hoop-back Windsor. It has a six-spindle back. Of great importance in determining whether a chair is valid or a reproduction is making sure that the four leg turnings and the turned arm supports are all turned the same.

Courtesy of Mr. and Mrs. John Merkle

Signed Thomas Hayward, this loop-back Windsor was made between 1815-1830 in Boston, Massachusetts. The seat is of poplar while the spindles are probably hickory. It is of the then popular bamboo design.

Courtesy of Mr. and Mrs. John Merkle

It was a common and acceptable practice to use an armchair Windsor in two ways besides simply as a chair. The first was to cut a center portion of the seat out and use it as a potty chair. The other was to turn it into a rocking chair such as the loop-back arm chair Windsor pictured here. Comfort was contingent on construction. Thus the number of spindles and the cant of the legs were of value then to those who sat, and of value now to those who invest. Notice also the double wedge construction.

Tavern Windsor

Courtesy of Mr. and Mrs. Dana Fertig

Yankee ingenuity was essential if the frontier was to be tamed, if the house was to become a home, if life was to become easier. Everything depended upon the individual. Thus, every once in a while one comes upon a furniture oddity, as is the case with this half seat Windsor. During the late seventeenth, eighteenth, and early nineteenth centuries the tavern and inn were the chief social institutions outside of the home and church. Along with the penny quart of beer, one could catch up on the latest news and gossip, philosophize over the most recent government events, and listen in on the important news of the day. And, if you were on the road, these eighteenth century ordinaries would feed and bed you down for a quarter, so that you were at least reasonably refreshed in the morning. At least, with two or three strangers sharing the same bed, you were assured of one thing — that there would be no shoes allowed in bed while sleeping.

The story goes that with inns being unable to contain the overflow of customers, especially at mealtimes, the one-half seat Windsor was developed. They took up less room and thus more chairs could be used and a larger group of people served. At any rate this mid-nineteenth century tavern Windsor is unique. I know of only one other.

40

From Maine comes this Sheraton or rod-back Windsor. To avoid getting the Shera-ton Windsor and the duck bill Windsor confused, simply look down the back of the chair. The duck bill will narrow down as the rods go into the seat in a distinctive duck's bill, as opposed to the rectangular back of the Sheraton. Notice the bamboo turnings which were fairly common, due to the Chinese influence on the American people during the early and middle eighteenth century. (c. 1820)

Shown is a loop-back Windsor of the early to mid-nineteenth century. Of unusual size, it is neither a true child's Windsor nor is it comfortable for an adult. It is probably of midwestern origin. The miniature chest is from Ohio. Dovetailed and on button feet, it makes a nice accessory.

Pennsylvania Plank Bottom

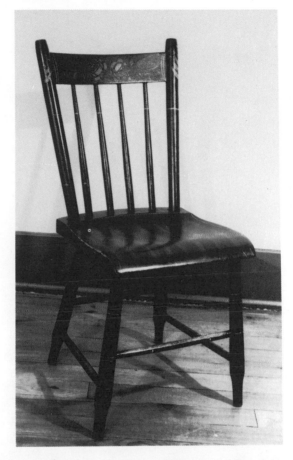

Plank bottom chairs can be placed in seven categories, all pertaining to their back construction. There is the angel back, half spindle, half spindle-thumb back, full spindle-thumb back, arrow back, balloon back, and bootjack. There can be any number of variations of the above. Also, a plank bottom is different from a Windsor because of the plank seat being scooped out across the seat rather than forming a saddle seat. These chairs, from Pennsylvania and dating from around 1830, were probably mass produced in a factory totally unfinished, and then the buyer would decorate at his discretion.

The background here is a black and red stripe over which has been painted the rose motife which seemed to be the favorite flower among the Dutch. The red-black stripe is carried through the plank bottom, while a yellow line encircles the rods and legs in several places. It is not unusual to find sets of plank bottoms in the original paint, but at the same time one must watch for "touchups" and RECENT complete repaintings. In the latter case the value may be considerably less.

Courtesy of Mr. and Mrs. Frank Clear

Here is a very fine half-spindle plank chair representing a set of four. It is not unusual to find sets of four or six today, and occasionally one comes across eight, ten, or twelve. Besides the turnings on the front rung and the half-spindles, notice the extra craftsmanship on the front legs, especially the small button feet. Made in Pennsylvania around 1825, it carries the stenciled rose motif on the top and center slat and also on the front of the plank. The flattened uprights are also decorated.

Pennsylvania Plank Bottom

Courtesy of Mr. and Mrs. Bruce Shultz

Receiving its name from the construction of the top slat, this half-rod, angel-wing back dates about 1825. It is of Pennsylvania origin. On the front rung and front legs are typical ring turnings, along with the knobs on the back half-spindles.

Hudson River Valley Rocker

Courtesy of Mr. and Mrs. Dana Fertig

Settled by the Dutch, the Hudson River Valley extends from Fort Orange (Albany) to New York City. As early as 1624, the Dutch West India Company had colonized New Netherland which was then part of the present states of New York, New Jersey, Connecticut, and Delaware. The great shipper and merchandiser, Cornelis Jacob May, in 1624 became one of the first permanent settlers in New Netherland. New York City was established in 1625. In 1626 the Dutch colonist purchased Manhattan Island from the Indians for 24 dollars worth of goods.

The Dutch joiners made their furniture heavy, but with graceful lines. Elaborateness, color, carving — all played an important part in creating furniture which would last. This ladder-back rocking chair is attributed to the Dutch of the Hudson River Valley. From the early eighteenth century, it not only has peg construction, but the shoe-foot rocker which has been worn almost flat. Also note the arm supports which are attached on the outside of the seat rung and set into the supporting leg rung. Note that the support of the leg rung has been cut as a part of the rung itself. As craftsmanship declined, the arm supports would run through the seat rung and into the leg rung, then finally just through the seat rung.

46

Early rockers are always exciting because they were totally a work of art, as opposed to the machine mass production of later years. This eighteenth century rocker is of Ohio origin. At first glance one's eyes rest upon the large bulbous turnings and short cradle-shaped stubby rockers. Notice also the rolled, recessed arm supports which go through to the first rung. In later rockers these supports, along with the bulbous turnings and the finial, would all be forgotten.

A New England child's rocker in the original red. (c. 1790)

Writing Arm Chair Rocker

This unique writing arm chair rocker is signed "R. Brierly." It is an Ohio piece from probably around the mid-nineteenth century. Although not greatly detailed as to craftsmanship, it does retain the original yellow outline trim and the leaf motif on the second and third slat. Notice also the convenient drawer under the 20¾ inch wide writing arm.

Courtesy of Mr. and Mrs. Frank Clear

Very rarely does one have the opportunity to purchase a five "rung" ladder-back rocker. The entire chair is hickory and from the first quarter of the nineteenth century. Notice the extension of the rockers in the rear, the pegged construction, and how the rockers are socketed to the legs.

Pennsylvania Mammy Bench

The whole idea behind the mammy bench was to allow the mother, or a "mammy," to rock a small child while at the same time allowing herself freedom to carry on another activity. While this one could be used as either a left or right handed mammy bench, there were those made as twin benches, where the mammy sat in the center, or a bench which had the "keeper" across the entire front. With the "keeper" removed the bench could be used as a rocking settee. This particular mammy bench, signed J. A. Sloss, retains the original flower and leaf stencil motif on the back rail and the fiddle-back splats. A slight chamfer on both ends of the rockers gives a finished effect. (1820-1830)

Indiana Mammy Bench

Courtesy of Mr. and Mrs. Frank Clear

One often wishes a piece could talk and give its life history. For that reason it is always exciting to find one like this arrow-back mammy bench. It has descended through the Newman family of Germantown (now Pershing), Indiana, and was made for that family in 1820. The "keeper" was somewhat unusual since there is only one hole in the bench. Thus, one end of the "keeper" would be placed there, while the other end would rest on the main supporting spindle of the arm.

Settles

The settle has always been a fascinating piece of furniture. It reminds one of a most primitive type of living coupled with the warmth of the early home. The high back and protruding bench ends functioned to keep off the drafts of the cold winter nights. Due to the lack of any sort of central heating, the fireplace was all important, so every effort was made to keep the warmth around the individual. The settle and its construction fulfilled that need. Settles were made in several forms. Some were slightly curved, with the back boards running vertically. Usually there was no bottom drawer or compartment. The back boards of straight settles were horizontal. Often under the seat was a compartment or drawer.

The late eighteenth century maple settle shown here is a variation of the earlier fireplace settle. Probably for the same purpose, it has a two-board seat which lends greater depth and more comfort. This and the wedged construction make this settle unique and easy to assemble or disassemble.

Wall Bench

It was not until 1700 that the joiner became the cabinetmaker. For all practical purposes, although his name changed, his tools did not. The bits were held in the planes through the pressure of wood; the lathe was turned according to the speed of his foot and all the material he needed for the furniture he created was only as far away as the forest.

Throughout the South during the seventeenth and early eighteenth centuries, the furniture in a small tobacco planter's cottage was simply several "forms" or benches, created by cutting a log in half and raising it to the desired height through the use of peg legs which may or may not have been wedged for strength.

However, with the urge for more functional pieces, and improved cabinetmaker skills, the bench was relegated to the kitchen, then to the summer kitchen, and finally its place was in the yard next to the well, used only at wash time by the men as they came in from the fields.

The wall bench shown is of Pennsylvania origin and retains its original graining. Note that as a wall bench it only needed a front apron, and the front side of each leg was cut out. Mortised, tenoned and single wedged, the legs are braced to the top board through the use of a triangular brace which makes it impossible to rock or sway.

"Wine Glass" Rope Bed

At Plymouth Plantation one comes across what may have been one of the first types of American beds, the "jack-bed." The bed was built into one corner of the log house. The head and side were supported by the house walls, and only one post was needed on the outer corner. Since one slept in a sitting position, there was really no need to sleep in a bed as long as one was tall. It was a long time between 1620 and about 1830 when this "wine glass" bed was made. Of Ohio origin, it received its name from the shaped knobs on the headboard and footboard which are of maple. The revolving blanket roll was for the convenience of the sleeper. All one had to do was pull the already rolled blanket off the roll for comfort.

Rope Bed

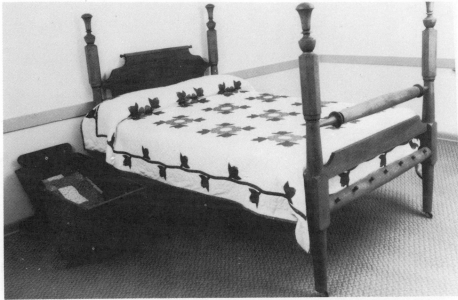

Courtesy of Mr. and Mrs. Frank Clear

The headboard and footboard are poplar while the posts are maple. This particular bed is of high quality due to the uniquely scrolled piece on the headboard and the octagon-sided posts. Commonly referred to as a three-quarter bed, it can be easily adapted to the full size mattress of today by adding four to six inches to the side rails. Dating about 1830, this bed is Ohio in origin.

New England Hooded Cradle

Shown here is an eighteenth century, hooded pine cradle retaining its original blue inside and original red outside. The hood conserved the warmth around the baby's head. The foot board is dovetailed while the headboard is nailed.

Mule Chest

One would suspect that the easiest construction and perhaps the most utilitarian piece of furniture would be of simple box construction. That is five pieces of wood pegged, dovetailed, or nailed together with a hinged top. What the box held depended upon its size. The size depended on the need and the ability of the workman to use tools and woods. The box pictured is of the middle eighteenth century and at that time would have been called a mule chest or donkey chest. Later it would be called a blanket chest. It was once stated rather colorfully of a donkey box —

"Over soaring mountains
Came courageous settlers,
Using these tough poplar boxes
For supplies.
Hung on the sides of donkeys
Or of mules,
Occasionally
They travelled
In their covered wagons.
Sometimes stuck in fords,
or roughly bounced
On rocky roads,
When sudden Indian ambush
Left whole families slaughtered.
Through such trials
And hardships
Came the Nation's birth,
For here were men
Who stood fast in their faith
And boldly said
'With Him as helper
I will never fear
What man shall do to me'."

This particular mule chest had its origin in New Hampshire. The construction is crude though there are some indications from the molded edge on the lift top and the single dovetailing on the drawer that there was some appreciation for a box which was just a little better. The drawer shows no indication of there ever being any type of pulls or knobs. It is made out of pine, the back board being 26 ½ inches wide and the front 17 ½ inches wide.

Immigrant Trunk

Shown is decorated Pennsylvania immigrant trunk signed M.F.D. and dated 1839. This type of trunk is not to be confused with the more highly decorated dower chest which usually was painted to resemble a three paneled chest and had the initials or name of the bride and the date of marriage.

Blanket Chest

Courtesy of Mr. and Mrs. Frank Clear

While the craftsmen and painters of the Mohontongo Valley in Pennsylvania produced some of the finest pieces of painted furniture, one cannot overlook the painted furniture from Lancaster, Berks, Montgomery, and Lehigh counties. Fine representative pieces also came from Ohio, New York, and the New England states. The "old blue" and the "Dutch red" seem to be the favorite colors for furniture, but occasionally one comes across pieces which have been smoke decorated. Attributed to Pennsylvania and probably of the early nineteenth century, this ball foot chest is dovetailed throughout and remains unique due to its smoked decoration of gold and black.

Blanket Chest

Shown is sponge decorated, Pennsylvania, one-drawer blanket chest. The bracket foot and the notched sides are typical of the 1830s.

Blanket Chest

Courtesy of Mr. and Mrs. Frank Clear

Typical of those chests made between 1830-1860, the one pictured is of Ohio origin and retains its mellowed red and green original color. Color was very important to the early home. Although in formal furniture it is the wood which is relevant to value, in country furniture, part of the value is found in the condition of the original paint. It should be pointed out that furniture prior to the late 1700s was not usually painted because wood seasoned correctly needed no paint.

In a real sense, paint did increase value to the early eighteenth century person. There are indications that paint was used in the home as early as 1734. One could not buy the paint desired, but had to mix it himself. Craftsmen learned that a combination of mineral substances would make a venetian red and vermilion. At the same time red paint was found to protect wood from deterioration. During the winter red on the barn absorbed the sun's rays and made the barn warmer. Red oxide of iron, skimmed milk and lime made a plastic-like coating that hardened quickly and lasted for years. When linseed oil was added the wood absorbed more of the paint. Indian red was made from clay mixed with the whites of turkey eggs. A deeper mahogany shade was made through the use of turkey blood. Green was made by adding crushed berries of dogwood or skunk cabbage, while the indigo plant juice created a blue color.

Ohio Blanket Chest

Designs were oftentimes painted on wood with a sponge. This poplar Ohio blanket chest is an example of that process. The red was painted on first, allowed to dry, and then the black was sponged on to give the effect of a pyramid side and a rectangular top. (c. 1830-40)

Pennsylvania Blanket Chest

Courtesy of Mr. & Mrs. Bruce Shultz

Although most Pennsylvania chests were built without drawers, a two or three drawer chest is not uncommon. However, a blanket chest with any drawers at all is becoming rather difficult to find. This raised panel, three drawer chest, retaining its original decoration, dates about 1820-1830.

Sheraton Chest of Drawers

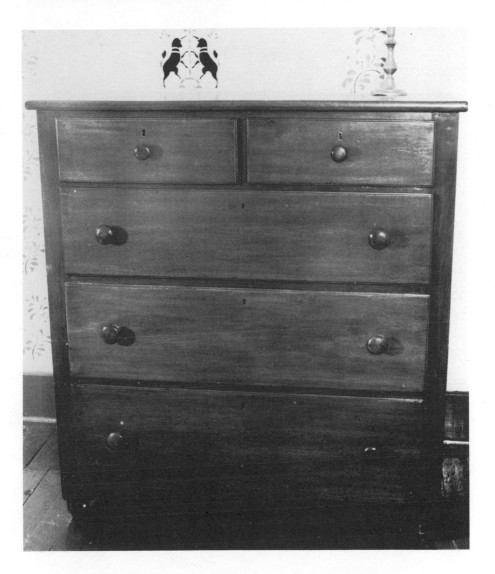

In the Sheraton style, this cherry chest has slightly graduated drawers, panelled sides, and thumbnail drawer molding. (c. 1820)

From the simple box to the chest of drawers is an evolution of time and craftsmanship. While at one time a trunk was all that was needed, later a chest of drawers was desired. As the styles changed in the cities, so did the country craftsman adapt his style in a limited way.

From Kentucky and of the Sheraton period (1795-1815), this chest of drawers indicates that the maker had some knowledge of what was popular in the metropolitan New England areas. The inlay banding was popular in Connecticut and northeastern Massachusetts, while the nicely graduated drawers with the thumbnail molding are indicative of the period. Note especially the signed period brass pulls. The beehive within the Christian church was the sign of St. Ambrose, the patron of bee-

keepers, and represented "many for the good of all." The symbol was adopted by the cabinetmaker with the words "nothing without labor" underneath. Chests like this also had the drawer bed running from front to back rather than from side to side as was the case with chests of a later period. Cherry is the primary wood with walnut being secondary.

The candlesticks are probably English and are developed in the full Rococo or Chippendale style. (1750-1775).

Vorschrifts (writing lessons) such as this one were common in the early school system. Being a very impressive piece of writing, it was given to pupils who were learning how to form numerals, capital and small letters in the German script and fractur writing. Often the creator's talents were shown off to the extent that letters were more decorative than legible. When the student had reached the same level of penmanship as the schoolmaster, the schoolmaster would oftimes present a Vorschrift to the pupil as a reward of merit and a token of his regard. Often in German and usually containing a moral lesson, the certificate would give the student something to live by through life. When translated this one states:

> "He who willingly takes a risk, Who becomes corrupt, an audacious person in the end is evil. Consider your activities before your death. Live so when you die you wish you had never lived otherwise. Hold in high esteem Father and Mother that you live long in the land the Lord thy God has given to you."

This particular Vorschrift was presented to Sammuel Konig in 1821 by Franz Syitler, Schoolmaster.

From Ohio and dating around 1830, the chest of drawers pictured looks rather cumbersome, due to its reverse order of graduated drawers. Usually the deepest drawer is the bottom drawer. Note the curved front foot which also detracts from its general appearance.

The small drawer on the right was usually considered the master's drawer. Thus the lock on that drawer would be different from the locks on the other four drawers. In it the master would keep valuable papers, plus other important family heirlooms which would ordinarily not be on display. Entirely of cherry, the chest has a valanced skirt that connects the turned legs. (c. 1820)

Pennsylvania Bucket Bench

This is one of the finest eighteenth century, Lancaster County, Pennsylvania, bucket benches. Its simplicity is superb. Notice the thumbnail molding on the front and rear of the top rail and the thickness of the wood. Total dimensions are 37" x 27 ¼ x 9".

Pennsylvania Bucket Bench

Courtesy of Mr. and Mrs. Harry Fertig

Of particular interest is this Pennsylvania bucket bench. Note the cut out, scrolled sides, the back splash board and the draining grooves on the top shelf. Mortised and tenoned throughout and in the original red, this bucket bench has all the traits that make it very desirable. (c. 1820)

The two gallon butter crock on the left was made by S. B. Bosworth in Hartford, Connecticut. It is unusual to have the word "butter" and the date 1884 on a butter crock. Incised "Somerset Potters Works," the crock at right was made either at Pottersville or Boston, Massachusetts, some time between 1882-1909. The unique cobalt blue handshake is a unusual design. S. Hart of Fulton produced the slip-cup double bird crock (on the floor) around 1870.

Ohio Bucket Bench

Within the limits of the preparation area once stood this Ohio bucket bench. Because of the top well, one might say this is a transitional piece, not a true bucket bench and not quite a dry sink. In the original green, it dates between 1830-1840.

The pine and hand-wrought iron well bucket is from the eighteenth century. By the second half of the nineteenth century, salt glazed stoneware began to decline — except in a few areas where there was a last great spurt of quill traced and cobalt blue glazed decorating. Between 1865 and 1870 the art of "pot painting" became a craze. The pecking chicken is from that era.

Sipe-Nichols and Company worked in Williamsport, Pennsylvania, until 1893. The crock pictured is from about 1865. The stoneware was made in a two story factory with a horse powered turnstile which supplied the power for the potters' wheels. The horses walked on the second story while the potters worked on the first. It is interesting that here, as in other stoneware factories, girls operated the wheels to throw, glaze, and stamp the stoneware. Their names were never recorded.

Illinois Bucket Bench

One of the major concerns of the settlers was water supply. In part this explains the proximity of early settlements to the rivers of America. The homestead was either built on top of a well, as with the Plimpton House, or a well was within a short distance. The well buckets were filled each morning before the day's work began and each evening before retiring, so that one would not be caught short during the day or night. The buckets filled with drawn water would be placed on what we know today as a bucket bench, a descendant of the common wash bench. It was usually made up of two or three shelves. The upper shelf was where the fresh water buckets were placed when filled, and the bottom shelf was for storage.

Pictured is a mid-nineteenth century bucket bench from Illinois which is somewhat unusual as most bucket benches are of Pennsylvania origin. Very crude in style, it does retain its original blue color and has the unique feature of a soap and wash pan shelf below the first shelf.

Pennsylvania Bucket Bench

Courtesy of Mr. and Mrs. Frank Clear

Whether the item shown here is a dry sink or a bucket bench depends on what part of the country you are from. One would be inclined to call this a bucket bench because of the leg height from the floor, and the two smaller than usual doors.

Often one hears of a piece being "washed." This means there has been some minor restoration and the original color has been changed through the use of ammonia, so that the unpainted wood takes on the original color and thus blends with the rest of the piece. The value is not necessarily taken away when this is done, providing it has been done as a local restoration. However, if the entire piece has been painted or repainted, then we no longer have a restoration, but the next thing to a reproduction. The bucket bench pictured is from Pennsylvania, in the original red, and dates from around 1840.

The dry sink is one of the most popular pieces of country furniture. Originally, almost every country home had some variation of it. Among the low-backs were those without drawers, or with a right or left drawer which usually contained the culinary equipment most commonly needed. However, style again became important, and the simple dry sink became the high-back with either one or two shelves, more drawers, and a larger storage area.

One of the finest dry sinks is this Ohio high-back with double shelf. Simple and pleasing to the eye, it has all the construction characteristics which enhance its value: thumbnail molding around the drawers, extra notching on the side panel as it moves into the top shelf, chamfered door panels, mortised and tenoned throughout and retaining the original red along with some of the door stenciling — all these together, plus the double candle drawers, have created the finest. (c. 1820)

Courtesy of Mr. and Mrs. Frank Clear

Dating from around 1820, this poplar high-back dry sink has many characteristics which enhance its refinement. The brass knobs on the candle drawers, the two long knobs and locks, coupled with the exceptionally well chamfered door panels, unite to create a piece of beauty.

Courtesy of Mr. and Mrs. Frank Clear

This is a poplar high-back, single shelf dry sink of the mid-nineteenth century. Note the scrolled end boards, the mushroom pull and the molding on the right door which when closed hides the door seam.

Courtesy of Mr. and Mrs. Bruce Shultz

Shown is a fine example of an Ohio Amish, low-back dry sink. Of particular interest is the cut out bracket foot on both the front and side. Note that while most dry sinks were totally enclosed around the well, thus making the homemaker reach over the front into the well, this one is cut out at the front so that there is easier access to the working space. Also there is the slightly slanted and molded drain board. It is in the original red and dates from about 1820.

Pennsylvania Dough Trough

Although occasionally one still finds one, the opportunity to purchase a good dough trough is becoming less frequent. The one pictured was purchased at an Illinois farm sale but is of Pennsylvania origin. Mortised and tenoned throughout the leg structure, it rates among the best due to its being red and black wood grained. This technique of wood graining was practiced frequently in the nineteenth century. Any competent painter equipped with the graining tool could do it. This tool resembled a quarter cylinder with a raised series of lines. By dragging the tool through a layer of fresh paint over a dry undercoating the painter created an amazing resemblance to grained wood. A variation of this technique was comb painting. A comb-like device was dipped in fresh paint and then combed over a dry undercoating to leave a very fine, lined effect.

Ohio Dough Tray

Food preparation was essential to the pioneer family. Pieces had to be made to accommodate this demand. Two of the most popular would be the dough tray, which is pictured here, and the dough trough. The premise behind their development was that the cover of either piece became the kneading board for the dough, while the trough or tray became the rising compartment. It is quite common to find dough trays in the original red, although yellow is sometimes found. They are usually dovetailed at the corners and have small handles pegged into the ends. Those with handles as a part of the side boards are less common and consequently more desirable. Because their basic design remained the same over a period of years, it is difficult to place a date on them. Most trays and troughs which are found today are of the period between 1840-1860.

Sometimes pieces are found which at one time had a specific function, but now are questionable as to that function. Such is this fine New England hanging cupboard of the early 1800s. Without question the drawer at one time served as a spice container or salt box. The problem is the cabinet with its four mortised and tenoned racks. It is too small for a pewter spoon rack, too large for a pipe rack. Note the circular wire pulls, the detailed chamfered wooden skirt around the pane of glass, and the hand wrought hook. It measures 22" high, 6½" deep and 10¼" wide.

Hanging cupboards were created for individual situations, for just that right place in the home. Today they are sold to those who have just the right place. Whether the cupboard has a solid wood front or a glass panel, whether it has shelves or is composed of little drawers becomes secondary; it is the construction and age which become important. This New England eighteenth century hanging cupboard is desirable for its cock-bead molding, simple design, and age. With one shelf inside, it measures only 13 ¼ " high x 12" wide x 9 ½ " deep.

The Hussite Unitas Fratrum (Unity of Brethren) in Bohemia and Moravia grew out of fifteenth century Bohemia. In 1740 the Unity of Brethren moved to Bethlehem, Pennsylvania, from Herrnhut, in Saxony, and began the first American Moravian settlement in America. From Pennsylvania in 1753 a group of Moravians moved to Winston-Salem, North Carolina, and founded a second community united through a spiritual life with good works and independence. The hanging cupboard pictured is from that settlement. Dating from around 1790-1810, it retains the two side hanging hooks, the original lock and key, and butt hinges. Note the fine cornice and typical Moravian molding on the crest. Inside are two six-inch-wide shelves and a drawer with a leather pull. In the original red, it rates among the finest.

Pennsylvania Hanging Cupboard

Of Pennsylvania origin, the hanging cupboard pictured dates about 1840-1860. Judging from the shelf construction and the top molding, this may have been originally in a church. The shelf construction suggests that a communion chalice and flagon, plus prayer books, were stored there. The molding may be symbolic of the Trinity.

Corner Cupboard

Courtesy of Mr. and Mrs. Bruce Shultz

The corner cupboard, like the chimney cupboard, was built for a particular place which ordinarily could not be used by another type of cupboard. The triangular base permitted full use of the corner for storage. While some are in two sections, this particular cupboard is of one section and entirely of cherry. A more formal cupboard would have small-paned glass upper doors, possibly a notched spoon rack on the upper shelves, and a more decorative molding. (c. 1820)

Exciting pieces of furniture are still available in their original habitat, as this corner cupboard illustrates. Found several months ago in a log house near Hendersonville, North Carolina, it displays some rather interesting features. It can be used either as a corner cupboard, because its sides are diagonal, or it can be a wall cupboard as its back is flat. Note that the spoon rack, which is usually in the front of Pennsylvania and New England cupboards, is at the rear of the shelves, which may be a construction trait representative of the area out of which it came. Also, it is unusual to find a cupboard which combines leather hinges and butt hinges. Jack planed throughout and in the original green, this piece is truly country and from the early nineteenth century.

Shown is a combination cheese safe and jelly cupboard of Norwegian origin. It is in the original red. Note the apron on both the top and the bottom. Tradition has it that the raised panels were usually on the outside of the cupboard doors, due to the Norwegian feeling that a cupboard door should be closed, thus showing the craftsmanship. In much Pennsylvania construction, the door is to be left open, and thus the chamfering is on the inside. (c. 1820-1830)

A cupboard is any piece of furniture used for storage. Today we find any number of jelly cupboards, pie cupboards, cheese cupboards, corner cupboards, chimney cupboards, clothes presses, pewter cupboards, and wall cupboards. They may come in one or two pieces, with or without glass panels, with wood panels or solid doors. Their moldings may be from a straight right angle to half round, quarter round, torus, cyma recta, or a very intricate variation of any of these. Good early cupboards are in demand, expensive and difficult to find.

Pictured is a late eighteenth century cupboard of Ohio origin. Completely original throughout, it is mortised and tenoned, has long wooden pull and latch knobs on top and bottom, and a small but convenient pie shelf. Of particular interest is the jack planing on the inside of the doors.

Common thought has it that during spring or fall housecleaning, a new coat of paint was applied on the furniture. This is questionable. It is not unusual to find a piece such as this one which has the original red over the original blue. Two coats of paint over 175 years is a far cry from a fresh coat each year.

Courtesy of Mr. and Mrs. Frank Clear

Here is another Ohio one-piece wall cupboard dating between 1800-1830. The small pie shelf and the great apron are especially distinctive. Made of poplar with chestnut panels, it retains its original red on the outside and the original green on the inside.

Stenciled on the jug is "Samuel Felt, Jr., Druggist, Watertown, New York." Upon investigation it was found that Samuel Felt purchased the Nicholis N. Smith Drug Store on Court Street in 1883. However, there were no potters in Watertown at this time, so the jug must have been made to order by an outside potter.

Courtesy of Mr. and Mrs. Bruce Shultz

From Ohio, this one-piece, walnut wall cupboard is of nice proportion and construction. The raised door panels are superb, the pie shelf is wide enough to be useable, and the mitered moldings around the window panes correspond and thus hide the shelf sides. Dating between 1800-1820, it originally was built into a wall and ceiling. Thus there is no top molding and the pie shelf overhang on the right side is not present.

Courtesy of Mr. and Mrs. Frank Clear

Shown is a two-piece, walnut wall cupboard of the mid-nineteenth century. It is probably of Ohio origin.

Cheese-Jelly Cupboard

Courtesy of Mr. and Mrs. Frank Clear

Shown is a unique cheese-jelly cupboard combination. Within such a cupboard would be the winter's supply of canned fruits, meats, vegetables, jellies, and all of the other items which the homemaker worked so diligently at during the harvest season. The preserving of food was a must if one were to survive. Today we sometimes forget that there was no reliable vacuum canning in glass until the 1860s. There were no ice refrigerators and no refrigerated transporting of meat until the 1870s, and glass cost too much until the 1880s for the average homemaker to buy. Notice the bracket base and the large cornice, unusual on ordinary jelly cupboards. (c. 1820-1840)

Chimney Cupboard

In the large family of cupboards were the chimney cupboards. Their narrowness was due to their being placed in a narrow space between the side of the fireplace and the wall. Many early homes had built in chimney cupboards for clothes as the heat from the fireplace would retard moisture and mildew. This cupboard is from Hershey, Pennsylvania. Jack planed throughout, it retains its original two wooden catches, mushroom pull and red paint. (c. 1830-1850)

Schoolmaster's Desk

Courtesy of Mr. and Mrs. Frank Clear

Was this a schoolmaster's desk or a blacksmith's desk? Was it a storekeeper's desk or was it a desk at all? It is entirely of walnut and from the mid-eighteenth century. It probably never saw a home until it was classified as an antique. It seems to be more of a lectern than a desk because the writing arm surface is too high and the box too deep to sit at. A more practical solution for a writing desk was to hinge the lid at the base so as to have a flat and lower writing surface. This was accomplished 100 years before this desk was made, but furniture design is by people. We make advances, but at times we also make a decision toward the impractical.

Yarn Winder

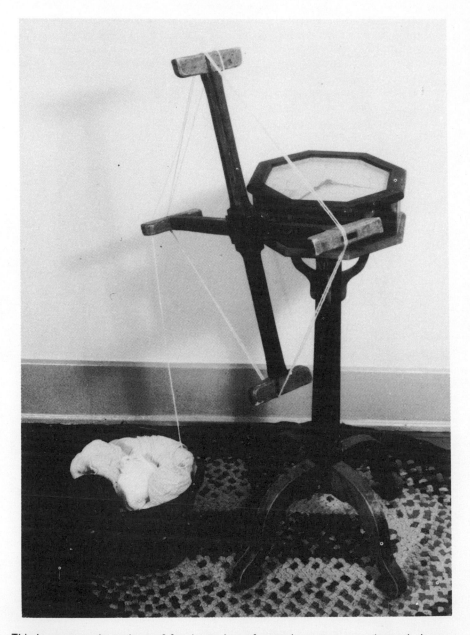

This is not exactly a piece of furniture, but of great importance to the early household was the yarn winder. The winder usually consisted of four or six arms positioned in a two yard or one and one-half yard circumference. The wool winder served the function of accurately winding the cotton or wool into skeins. A skein of cotton consisted of eighty turns of the thread upon a 54'' winder. In winding wool eighty turns would equal one knot, and a skein of wool would be equal to seven knots. With this use in mind, the yarn winder takes on considerable importance to the collector. Beginning with the octagon clock encasement which holds a complete wooden clock works, right down through the supporting brackets and the octagon pedestal, this simply constructed piece takes on very pleasing characteristics. The clock dial has two hands, one small, one large, which circulate clockwise on a numbered background. The large hand goes one full digit, equaling one turn or two yards on the winder, while the small hand records the number of knots. A New England piece, it dates from the early part of the nineteenth century.

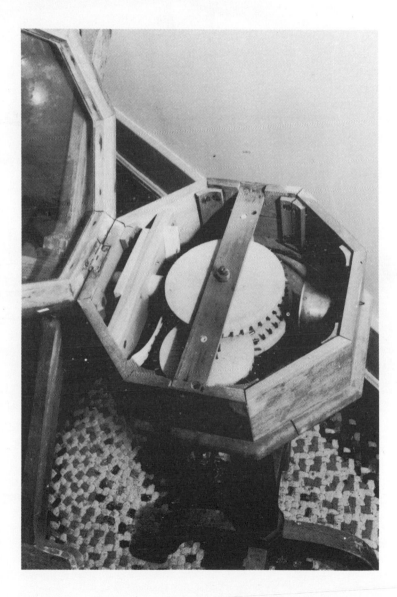

Candle Drying Rack

From New England and of the late eighteenth century, this candle drying rack could still serve its original function, that of allowing the candles to dry between dippings and before being stored for future use. In the "building up" process, about 32-35 dips would be needed to make a candle which would fit into a conventional candlestick. This process was slow, and ingenuity brought forth the candle mold which would quicken the candle making process.

Norwegian Rosemaling Trunk

The Norwegians assimilated with the Dutch after 1630 at New Amsterdam, Albany, and Schenectady to the extent that they were not only tradesmen but also they held public office. In 1740, a group of Norwegians joined the Moravian faith and founded the Bethlehem, Pennsylvania, colony. A Reverend Clausen and Governor Ramsey of Minnesota met in 1850, and the Norwegians were formally welcomed to settle in Minnesota, creating the first settlement in Goodhue County in 1851. Soon after Fillmore and Houston counties would be settled.

Much of the Norwegian furniture today comes from the old farm families of these counties. It is difficult to determine whether a piece was made in Norway and brought over, or whether it was made in America. Consequently, the point becomes almost irrelevant while the value remains constant.

The trunk pictured is extremely colorful due to the traditional rosemaling (painting) which was a peasant craft and flourished both in Norway and America during the eighteenth and nineteenth centuries. Dated 1811, it has the unusual feature of bracket-type feet, whereas most Norwegian trunks are flat on the ground.

Norwegian Rosemaling Trunk

The Norwegian trunk pictured is of unusual importance besides the fact of its beauty. During a period when it was expected that the average Norwegian family would have from eight to ten children, a trunk was made for each of the girls by either the father or a local craftsman. We know that this trunk was given to the second daughter by the fact that it has the number two on top of the escutcheon. We also know that this daughter was married in 1852 as that date is painted over the mother's wedding date of 1819.

Pennsylvania Settee

Courtesy of Mr. and Mrs. Frank Clear

A settee such as is pictured in Plate 2 was common in the Pennsylvania home in the first half of the nineteenth century. Commonly labeled a "deacon's bench," these were factory made and usually decorated to match a set of plank bottom chairs which were in the same home. Today it is rare that one finds the matching chairs and settee. The seat may vary from five to eight feet and have from six to ten legs. The spindle styles would be the same as for plank bottom chairs.

Room Settings

After one has observed and appreciated pieces separately as they are described in a book, it becomes important to see them in their total room setting. Perhaps we can be helpful in that area by presenting several room settings using those pieces which have been described.

The Keeping Room

The Summer Kitchen and Woodbox

The Master Bedroom